About the Author

Hello there! I'm the author of *'A Work In Progress'* and I currently live in Swansea with my mum and nan. As you will discover in this book, I suffer with my mental health quite badly and that has fuelled me to share my story to help others feel less alone, because mental health issues can make you feel very alone. Besides that I love books, beaches and coffee, which often make a great day out. I have a hugely supportive network of friends and family and can't thank them enough.

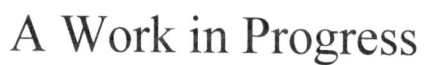

A Work in Progress

Elisha Harris

A Work in Progress

Vanguard Press

VANGUARD PAPERBACK

© Copyright 2023
Elisha Harris

The right of Elisha Harris to be identified as author of
this work has been asserted by her in accordance with the
Copyright, Designs and Patents Act 1988.

All Rights Reserved

No reproduction, copy or transmission of this publication
may be made without written permission.
No paragraph of this publication may be reproduced,
copied or transmitted save with the written permission of the
publisher, or in accordance with the provisions
of the Copyright Act 1956 (as amended).

Any person who commits any unauthorised act in relation to
this publication may be liable to criminal
prosecution and civil claims for damages.

A CIP catalogue record for this title is
available from the British Library.

ISBN 978 1 83794 079 0

*Vanguard Press is an imprint of
Pegasus Elliot Mackenzie Publishers Ltd.*
www.pegasuspublishers.com

First Published in 2023

**Vanguard Press
Sheraton House Castle Park
Cambridge England**

Printed & Bound in Great Britain

For those who believed in me and those who didn't, I can't thank you enough. Without you, there wouldn't be this book.

I would like to thank my mother, who has supported me throughout my process of writing this book. I'd like to thank my aunt and nan for being there with me for the subjects of my poetry. Also, to my past therapist Diane who was the first person I revealed my poetry to and experienced the magic of sharing such personal experiences. I'd like to thank the women in book club who have built me up as a person. And lastly I'd like to thank you for picking this book up. You have made a dream come true.

Contents

Love and light. 15
The man. 16
My lover. 17
Sunset on the horizon. 19
The fish and the elephant. 20
Wonderland. 21
Glasses. 22
Sugar and salt. 23
Sugar and spice. 24
Answers to anorexia. 25
You are too late. 26
Kindness. 27
Losing battle. 28
Domestic abuse. 29
Sacrifices. 30
A tortured land of love. 31
The music of your voice. 32
A doomed love. 33
The journey. 34
Ending. 35
Settling. 36
Rehearsals. 37
Lover. 38
Learning life. 39
Muted. 40
Church. 41
We are lost. 42

Used.	43
All you needed.	44
Lost.	45
Youth.	46
Writing.	47
A drug.	48
Lighting the fire.	49
Demons	50
What's the difference?	51
Yes.	52
Waiting for mermaids.	53
Poetry.	54
Masking.	55
Young and sweet.	56
Pink.	57
Darkness.	58
A) or B).	59
Education.	60
Red.	61
Wonderland part two.	62
An old soul.	63
Love.	64
Hostage.	65
False promises.	66
Trees.	67
Beauty within.	68
The sculpture.	69
My words or lack of.	70
Mother's love.	71

A fool's memories.	72
My pick 'n' mix.	73
Old days.	74
Safe person.	75
Therapy.	76
You're a garden	77
Yellow.	78
Safety.	79
Actions are our future.	80
My creation of you	81
Beauty.	82
The raw ache of a blade.	83
The first.	84
Want and need for seep of blood.	85
Contemplation.	86
The reason	87
Monsters.	88
Is it my final dance?	89
Zebra.	90
Protected.	91
Dark clouds.	92
Hospital canteen	93
A spoon.	94
The same bark	95
Anorexia's hold.	96
Discovery.	97
Just a girl.	98
What I know.	99
Falling.	100

Claiming or changing	101
A depression wave	102
Borderline Personality Disorder	103
I am a poet	104
A lifetime within three days.	106
Satisfaction	107
Poetry	109
Just a dream	110
This changed me	111
Weirdly wonderful world	112
Beach	113
Possibilities of the beach	114
Proof of toothache	115
Musical transportation	116

Love and light

The love we once had,
Still has the power,
To light even the darkest
Of hours.
While the love we now have,
Has the power,
To darken even the brightest
Of hours.

The man

As a child I was the property of
My father.
As a teen I was the property of
My first love,
Who held my heart in his palm
Moments away from being
Crushed.
As an adult I was the property of
My husband,
Who was paid more than I.
As I grow old, fragile, I am the property of
My son.
Who visits monthly and tells me of the promotion he received over
The women who sacrificed a family for
That job.

My lover

The first time I saw my lover,
I fell in love with the way her words grew closer with
excitement,
The way her hair parted to the right,
The hop in her walk,
The way she licked her lips before talking.

Two years we were together
Minus the 'growing time'
Which equalled twenty-eight days.

The countless anniversaries,
Missed.

We experienced in our period together
Three marriages, five babies, two houses, and four deaths.
None ours. Nothing brought us together.

As life moved fiercely, so did we.

I ended up resenting the way her words would grow
quicker with excitement, the hair perfectly parted to the

right, her bunny hop, and the way she licked her lips before each word.

I resented her and mourned our once love.

Sunset on the horizon

As the ball of fire,
Slowly kissed the glass
Surface of the sea,
A radiant glow erupted
Filling the summer sky.
The one where we first experienced
Our first kiss under.

The fish and the elephant

I wish I had the memory of the fish
Instead of the elephant.
As each night,
I lay reliving our days
Looking for what I did wrong and what I could change.

Wonderland

I wish I lived in Wonderland
Where the food has labels saying "eat me" with endless tea parties.
But instead, I live in this tortured unknown land where each food I see,
I hear a voice saying, "Don't eat that."

Glasses

"Four eyes" they called me,
Little did they know.
I saw what others missed.
The steamy affair between Mrs June and Mr Ford.
The boy who had bruises everywhere.
The girl who cowered away at every man's touch.
They boy who only liked boys when playing kiss chase.
The girl who always said no to food.
I saw what society refused to see.
What society ignored.

Sugar and salt

You disguised yourself as sugar.
Sweet. Familiar, like the candy I ate as a child.

During our days, weeks that turned into months and
months that became years. Time wasting. Energy wasted.
Myself, wasting.

Finally, you became real. Revealing yourself.
Salt disguised as sugar.
Sour. Bitter. Sharp.

However, I always preferred the taste of salt.

Sugar and spice

Sugar and spice. They say we're made of all things nice.
Beauty. Sparkles. Glitter.
But also, defiance. Anger. Strength. Resilience.
Intelligence. Power.
Portrayed as the sex made of glass. Fragile. Delicate.
But glass can be mended, shaped and rebuilt.

Answers to anorexia

They say I look drawn,
"Like a picture of health," I say.
They say my heart is under too much stress,
"At least it's beating," I say.
They say my leg muscles are gone,
"At least I still have them," I say.
They say I'm playing Russian roulette,
"At least I'm winning," I say.

You are too late

An absent father can never be a father
As you lost the years to care and
Nurture for my child self.
You are too late
For I have learnt to stand alone.

Kindness

"It's not you, it's me,
You deserve better.
I don't want to hurt you"
But all you did was kill me with your
Idea of kindness.

Losing battle

You wrapped me up
In cotton wool
Now I am too fragile for this life.
A flower battling the harshest of
Weather.
I lost the battle of life as you killed me with your
Kindness.

Domestic abuse

I hate you.
You poor excuse of a man.
Fury.
Fire burnt in his eyes.
Whack.
He struck my mother.
My passion and defiance ran red from her nose.
I grew strong and independent
While my mother was belittled to the ground.

Sacrifices

I clawed up the ladder of success
Only to sacrifice what I never knew
I would want,
A family.

A tortured land of love

You live in an ignorant bliss.
Unknown to you, my love for you
Keeps me in a tortured land.
For you will never know as I will never have the courage
to tell you
Or let you in.

The music of your voice

Your voice is music to my ears.
Caressing me.
Unzipping the back of my dress.
I have no control, I always end up letting you in.

A doomed love

Your voice sends chills down my body,
For all the wrong reasons.
As we are in a doomed love,
And this is reality.
Where true love's kiss will not save
Us all.

The journey

The fear I feel,
Only brings you,
Closer to me.

Ending

My fear of death, pain and oblivion
Is crippling and brings you nearer.
I am my own end.

Settling

Should I have settled long ago?
As I'd not be chasing my desires now.
But I would be in a loveless marriage,
With children.
Not knowing how to truly love.

Rehearsals

Why did we have to rehearse our final
Scene so many times?
We tried so hard to change the script,
For the ending to be unchanged,
And for it to be our final curtain call.

Lover

Your girlfriend, lover and friend
I wanted to be…
Not your mother.
The time I spent running around after you,
Changed me.
My laughter faded, myself wasting and you left
For I had changed
And had no trace for who I once was.
You took me away.

Learning life

They bought me a fish,
A companion.
I waited for it to die,
To dissect it and see
What made it alive.

Muted

They say we need to take more
Interest in society,
Yet, they mute our voices.
And take no interest in us.

Church

Power.
Control.
Dominance.
That's what you practice.
Preaching for us to be perfect.
Your voice fills the walls with stories
Of death, hell, and eternal damnation.
Countless marriages failed,
Christenings producing devils,
And deaths filling hell.
As I turn each page,
I hear the screams
Of the supposed
Sinners.

We are lost

Countless news channels
With one thing in common,
Humanity is lost.

Used

I was the gift shop
Never the museum.

The pit stop
Never the destination.

All you needed

You didn't need to touch me.
Yet, you were able
To make me feel
Dirty,
Vulnerable,
Violated,
And used.

And all you needed was
A camera phone, changing rooms, and lastly
A child.

Lost

Innocence
Once lost
Can never be bought back.

Youth

Your little body filled with
Innocence, happiness, love, hope.

I only wish I could have an ounce of it now.
I wish I had protected you more.

Writing

The art of writing is a
Sweet cruel gift.

A drug

My body a drug
One of recreation to you
And one of medical to me.

Lighting the fire

The reason he will call you hot
Before beautiful is because
You enlighten a fire within him.

Demons

We are taught to fear others
Demons
Yet, it is our demons we should truly fear.
It's our demons that will hurt us.

What's the difference?

There is a difference between
Living and simply existing.

Yet, I don't truly know the difference.

Yes

Can you be dead with a
Beating heart?
With oxygen in your lungs?
And blood in your veins?

The answer is yes.

Waiting for mermaids

As I pick up the shell and bring it to my ear listening to the waves,
Waiting, for the mermaid
That I'd watch in the sea on those
Endless summer nights
Waiting to pick up.

Poetry

Literature is like a house,
A house with many rooms.
And I always find myself in the same room.
Poetry, my favourite and forever room.

Masking

What would people say
If they knew
The truth
Behind every
Smile and "I'm fine."

Would they still walk away smiling?

Young and sweet

My coming-of-age story
Was the same of me as a child
Being supervised to
Eat,
Sleep,
And even use the toilet.

Was I really young and sweet turning seventeen?

Pink

The colour that surrounds you is
Pink.
Filled with warmth, maternal love and care.
Yet, you still have a fire in your belly one fuelled by love
    and passion.
You show me not only to be pretty in pink,
But also strong, brave and courageous in pink.

    — Rainbow Part One.

Darkness

You are never truly alone in darkness.
Not only is the room filled with your lingering thoughts.
But you will be haunted with
Ghosts of your past.
The past versions of you.

A) or B)

What is worse?

a) There is no God and we are alone
or
b) There is a God and he allows all of this to happen?

Education

I know how to do my timetables,
analyse language,
dissect an animal heart.

Yet, I don't know how to love myself.

Red

A colour of love to one.
And anger to another.

— Rainbow, Part Two.

Wonderland part two

I'm glad I don't live in wonderland where the food has labels like "eat me" because temptation is cruel, and my tortured land can't get worse.

An old soul

A reader has lived the lives of hundreds.

Love

Love is so much more than two people.
It's a room filled with red, pink, yellow and orange.
A room filled with fire surrounding us.
Our bodies burning,
Yearning for each other's touch.
Hearts racing,
Protruding our chests.

Love is so much more than you and I.
So much more than happiness and that giddy feeling.
Love was happiness, excitement, warmth.
But that was before
Now it's sadness, fear and cold.
You changed the meaning for me,
The colours surrounding it, the desire for it.

Hostage

I hold my thoughts hostage
Afraid one will escape
And change the way you look at me.
I couldn't have you look at me that way.

False promises

You promised me control,
Yet, I have none.

You promised me beauty,
Yet, I have none.

You promised me happiness,
Yet, I have none.

You promised me friends,
Yet, I have none.

You promised me a life,
Yet, I am just a beating heart.

For the girls in my anorexia rehabilitation group, you know who you are.

Trees

People are like trees
No two the same shade.

Beauty within

They say beauty is both inside as well as out,
And that is why you have the prettiest of faces,
And the warmest of souls.

The sculpture

People are like clouds
Each one sculpted differently.

My words or lack of

My silence
Speaks louder
Than any words I could say.

Mother's love

You are never too old
For the warm love of
Your mother.
For her touch,
For her love.

A fool's memories

I was a fool
To make memories
With you,
Because now I'm tortured.
And I wonder is it you I miss
Or the you in my memories.

My pick 'n' mix

You ask me to remove my mask
But my mask is simply my face.
Shall I take it off and reveal my
flesh?
Because there is no 'real' me
Only a pick 'n' mix of what I want you to see.

Old days

I now miss the days of being anxious
Because now all I feel is
Fear and fright.

Safe person

You don't always need a place to feel
Safe.
Sometimes, it is just
A person.
Sometimes, it is you.

Therapy

The same room can make you feel
Safe or scared or both at the same time.
But you'll never realise it until you sit in that
Therapy chair.

You're a garden

You may feel like dirt on inside
Yet flowers grow out of you,
Revealing your beauty.

Yellow

You are the sun and the stars
Providing light in my darkness.

I was your sunshine but now you are mine.

    — Rainbow, Part Three.

Safety

When you leave,
Like they all do.
A piece of my safety,
Will too.

But that's okay,
Because at least I got to feel it.

Actions are our future

Words and promises are false hope
Yet actions are the concrete of the
Future.

My creation of you

You are not real.
I made you out of my words, love, care and warmth.
You are perfect to me.
But only exist to me.

Beauty

Beauty is around us
Because its within us
And it's what we project
And that is why everything around you
You see the beauty
In the trees,
Sky,
Mountains,
Sea,
And every little thing.
Because that beauty is within you.

The raw ache of a blade

It itches and aches
A raw ache
Where I want to run the blade
Where I want to see the blood run
And trickle constantly.

The first

That bittersweet curse
of the cut
and drop of blood.

Want and need for seep of blood

I want to—
No,
Wait.
I need to.
I need to feel
That blade.
Across my skin.
To see the blood,
Seep through my skin.

Contemplation

I sat on that bench at that beach
Contemplating it all.
My past and future life all rushing
Around my head.
Whether or not to stay for my future.

The waves more violent than
The voice in my head
Telling me to end it all.

The reason

That voice.
Soft and gentle,
Filled with love, warmth and familiarity.
That voice that reminded me I had more to live for than
I did to die for.

Monsters

My stomach roared louder
Than any monster under my bed.

But I learnt not to be afraid of the monsters
Under my bed but the ones in my head.

Is it my final dance?

I dance between the fine line
Of life and death.

Zebra

Your wild stripes
Echo my thoughts.
Wild,
Black and white,
With a hint of innocence.

Living with a land of danger
Just like the life around me.
The risk of being chewed up
Spat up
And left alone and vulnerable.

Protected

You protect the life in me.
Leaving me flourish, bloom and
Replenish.
But like everything
It does not last forever
And soon the bright, beautiful layers,
Turn to the deadly darkness.
And all that flourished
Is gone.

Dark clouds

Depression is the cloud
And the rain drops my suicidal thoughts.
Sometimes it rains.
Sometimes it pours.

Hospital canteen

An hour may be a long time
A short time.
But it's definitely not long enough
When it's all you get in a hospital canteen
With your mum.

A spoon

Three months have gone
And as I stir my coffee.
The outline of the spoon,
Reminds me of your body.
Your curved spine as you lay sleeping
On my bed.
Little did I know that would be the last time.
Now my mind is filled with you
And even a spoon reminding me of you.

The same bark

The same bark
Can either make you the tree or
The dog.

Anorexia's hold

I didn't have anorexia,
Anorexia had me.

Plucking each of my bones to the surface.
Ripping the life out of my body,
Slowly and steadily.
Every ounce of me fading away
Slowly,
From the hairs on my head to
The laughter I once
Had.

Discovery

I was meant to discover
My true self in university.
Yet, it was discovered in a
therapy chair.

Just a girl

My body ached for your touch.
It roared for your love.
Yet, when you finally touched me
My body became alive
A fire erupting in it.
Because I was just a girl
In love.
And your love, your touch was too much,
Too powerful.

What I know

I write about myself.
Not because I am selfish
Nor self-absorbed
But because it's the subject
I know the most
And least about.
It fascinates me most.

Falling

I fell.
I fell down a rabbit hole,
Like Alice did.
And I woke up at a cliff top,
Contemplating it all.

Claiming or changing

I claim to be a different girl now.
And yes, to some extent I am.
I didn't use a blade this time.
But a scissors worked just as well.

Yet, I am a different girl as I put down the scissors there was instant regret, a tear and pain.
I saw my mother's face and felt the guilt of hers and not mine this time, although it was there, my guilt is always there from my first and will be there for my last cut.

A depression wave

My depression is turning into a machinal wave machine.
Each one ready to come before the one before has come.
I am prepared. Ready. Yet, I still fear drowning and do come quite close to drowning each time. But then I remember all I need to do is ride the wave till the water is calm and steady.
And just as I ride it the next wave comes and I am left drowning, waving my hands in the air, gasping and screaming. Waiting for the calm.
It's like the calm before the storm. Except there is no end in sight for this storm as it will keep coming and coming and coming until maybe one day I do drown.
Maybe one day my end will come as I wave my hands in the air, gasping and screaming. Slowly losing the battle with a machine-like depression.

Borderline Personality Disorder

BPD. A three-letter abbreviation for an illness that is so much more than illness so much more than three letters.

Give it its full title BORDERLINE PERSONALITY DISORDER.

It is so much more than a disorder or a personality trait it's an illness that kills, it's the modern-day cancer. Can suicide be a modern-day cancer or AIDS?

It is unspoken about, it lurks in corners of rooms where people sob in pain silently or crying under covers, afraid to talk or mention the words depression, anxiety, BPD.

I am a poet

I sit at my desk typing away like a pianist at their piano.
Each letter hits the spot differently.
Clicks differently.
Impacts differently.

I am a poet, and the keyboard is my piano.
I am a poet, and life is my muse.
I am a poet, and experience is why I write.

Scratches

I lost two and a half years for six scratches on my arm. Eight hundred forty-four days of proud that I was clean from self-harm.

And now I am panicked and worried how to get to one day clean.

But the same way I got to eight hundred forty-four days I will take a day at a time and keep moving forward. Slowly, taking minute by minute, day by day and week by week, and the year by year.

This time I will make it till the end of time without another self-made scratch on my arm.

A lifetime within three days

Within three days
I fell in love
And out of love
Then back in love with life.

I went from being okay
To crying and praying to die
To being relieved to be alive.

BPD can change your view on life
Minute by minute,
Hour by hour,
Day by day.

But at least I stick around every time to see it change.

Satisfaction

Curiosity killed the cat,
Satisfaction brought it back.
But I'm not a cat and satisfaction will not bring me back
To the girl
Who loved, wholeheartedly
With every inch of her being
And every inch of her soul.
Satisfaction just might kill that girl
But bring another.

A Wise and Old Soul

Sitting on her bed
Listening to Arctic Monkeys on repeat
Constantly hoping her soul will be as cool
And youthful
As her music taste

But in reality, she is just an old and wise soul
With pretty good taste in music.

And some things don't need to be changed, just like her
    soul doesn't,
Nor the music taste.

Poetry

Words running into lines into stanzas
But is that just it?
Similes, adjectives, nouns?

Because to you and I it's so much more,
It's a love language.
It's our communication.
And just as your hands unzip my dress so your words
undress my mind.
And just as hands run through my hair so your words run
through my head.

Just a dream

'It was all a dream' lights up in neon lights in my room
and as I close
My eyes.
I still see the neon pink lights in my eyelids.
A voice repeating it was all a dream
It was all a dream
It was all a dreammmmmmmm.

And sometimes I'm thankful it was just a dream
But then sometimes I wake up slightly heartbroken and sad
Because it was just that
A dream.

This changed me

What changed you?
I can tell you exactly what changed me.
A few self-help books, a book club
And a few strong women
With advice I will take with me through life
With laughter I will hold in my heart
With knowledge I will keep in my brain
And with kindness I'll treasure forever.

Weirdly wonderful world

I used to feel so alone, so very alone
In a big and scary world
I felt so little
A voice no one really listened to you.

But that's all changed.
Whether I'm alone or not,
And whether this world is big and scary,
Whether I'm so little or not.
I'm a voice that's really listened to.

And this world is weirdly wonderfully big in a way
I can get lost in a person's eyes and words,
And it's scary in a way I could live a life with endless possibilities
And isn't it incredible I'm so little that I can fit in a plane and fly and explore this weirdly
Wonderful
World,
That I have the pleasure in sharing with
You.

Beach

I want to go to the beach
Feel the heat and sun beam on my face
The sand under my hands, each grain drifting through my fingers as I watch it group by my feet.
And when I slowly get up and walk towards the glistening water, reflecting
A blue sky with few and far white pearly clouds between
Dipping my feet in the warm water my cares wash away with each wave
And I am free like a bird
No cage in sight
Just me at peace with the world
Just me dipping my feet in the sea with sand on my hands and sun on my face.

Possibilities of the beach

I can now picture myself on the beach
And see all the beach has
All its wonders, warmth and loveliness.
Without thinking shall I walk in, walk under the water,
Into an oblivion?

Because now my answer is no, I shall not.
I shall sit there with the warmth on my cheeks pulling my
 freckles to the surface.
Sit there enjoying the wonders of the sea, debating if there
 is such thing as a mermaid.
And I will swim under the water and hold breath, but I will
 come up for air and feel alive and free and born again,
As the water turns my hair curly with sea salt.
And I'll stay there until sunset.
And I will remember and hope there is a tomorrow that can
 just be as
Lovely.

Proof of toothache

I remember having anorexia like toothache, the dull constant pain
The not being able to get away from it, a break nor distraction from it
And like toothache I know it can come back short and sharp,
But just as I take care of my teeth
I now take care of mind, heart and soul.
And like I don't have toothache everyday
I don't have anorexia everyday
Because I can distract myself and have a break and I can get away from it
The dull constant pain is gone.

And I'm living proof it goes.

Musical transportation

Music like words has the ability to transport a person
As I lay on my bed listening to music and close my eyes
I'm happy and carefree dancing again in a field with like-minded people
Just in the moment of freedom,
Good music, bad dancing, and kind people
And then I open my eyes and I'm transported back to my room, writing poetry.